Sheila Malloy-Hall

Chandelier & **Suicide**

My Darkest Day Turned Glorious at the End of a Cord

Sheila Malloy-Hall

Redemption's Story Publishing, LLC, Houston, Texas (USA)

Chandelier & Suicide:
My Darkest Day Turned Glorious at the End of a Cord

Copyright © 2019
Sheila Malloy-Hall

Editor:
Angela Edwards
www.PearlyGatesPublishing.com

All Rights Reserved.
No portion of this publication may be reproduced, stored in any electronic system, or transmitted in any form or by any means (electronic, mechanical, photocopy, recording, or otherwise) without written permission from the publisher. Brief quotations may be used in literary reviews.

Print ISBN 13: 978-1-947445-70-3
Digital ISBN 13: 978-1-947445-71-0
Library of Congress Control Number: 2019909194

For information and bulk ordering, contact:
Redemption's Story Publishing, LLC
Angela Edwards, CEO
P.O. Box 62287
Houston, TX 77205
RedeemedByHim@Redemptions-Story.com

Dedication

I must preface this by stating I am not out to hurt anyone's reputation. I'm telling my story as it happened to me (or as best as I can recall by overhearing others *discuss* **ME**).

While penning this book, I was enduring a season of character-building. Putting my fingers to work as I typed away meant that I would truly stretch myself beyond what I've known my capabilities to be. From this point forward, I must own up to everything I have been saying to both myself and others, especially since my motto has become, *"Tell your story so no one else can. Tell your story the way that **ONLY YOU** can – all while facing your fears."*

Chandelier & Suicide was very necessary. I have come to a place in my life's journey where there was a process that needed to happen so that I could progress to that "next season." The realization that me telling my truth would prepare me for what's next continued to push me toward completion…letter by letter. One thing I know for sure is that if I don't tell my story, somebody else will!

I believe the universe has opened the doorway for me, as there are many who need to know my truths and be encouraged to live and fight another day. I have no doubt the enemy is going to use others to discourage me by calling me names, rejecting and abandoning me, and so forth and so on. I cannot concern myself with that right now. I must do what is necessary…for **ME**. So, as I pen and share my story, I am (admittedly) doing so with shaky knees coupled with the utmost confidence in my obedience to Christ.

I would first like to dedicate *Chandelier & Suicide* to **MYSELF** for facing this character-building exercise. I am super-proud of me, where I've been, where I am, and where I'm going.

Secondly, I dedicate this book to my husband, **Welton Hall**. With all honesty, I can say that without his support, I don't know if I would have pursued my literary venture in this season. Welton has been my biggest cheerleader and the man who stood in the gap for us so that I could do what needed to be done. During my season of building, he, too, was thrown into a season of his own. His faith, patience, and understanding were challenged, and I am very appreciative of how he stood by my side. Welton, I love you more than mere words could ever express!

Prologue

"SHE" is the nickname that was given to me growing up. (I believe it's safe to assume that "SHE" is short for Sheila.) I'm unsure who first gave me the name "SHE," but it quickly grew on me. I liked it then…and I **LOVE** it now!

Allow me a moment to introduce myself.

My name is Sheila. I am sharing with you as much as I can recall of my life's story (there are some things I don't remember or simply do not know). Therefore, some of the information or events that will be shared will contain bits I've learned from others' accounts of my life. However, that is not going to stop me from divulging my story in ways I've never done before.

Chandelier & Suicide contains my **VERY** real, **VERY** raw, and **VERY** awful struggles. Don't stop reading, though! There are also funny and bittersweet moments that comprise the very essence of "SHE"! Without reservation, you will read about both the good and bad decisions I've made. Some things will be utterly shocking to you, but know that everything I share is **VERY** intentional.

I invite you, my friend, to journey with me as I share with you the different seasons of my life. I've been completely broken, unsure of my identity, mistreated, sexually violated, depressed, suicidal, and so much more. As you travel with me, you will see that your state of brokenness is temporary. You can and **WILL** recover—but it's not without some work, ups and downs, and challenges along the way. You will come to learn you have strength and courage of which you were likely unaware. Then, as you come to the close of journeying through my seasons, you will find that through it all, **I SURVIVED! I'M STILL STANDING!** I take full ownership of my life's story and refuse to give that power to anyone else!

Now, I won't be able to share every single little moment of my life (that would require a second book—and I don't foresee myself doing that). Nonetheless, the beginning, middle, and end of my seasons are sure to be riveting and thought-provoking!

I'm hopeful that the lessons I share in this book will set others free and propel them to fulfill their God-ordained purpose.

I cannot stress enough that this book is **NOT** intended to hurt or betray anyone. This is **MY** story. This is what happened to **ME**. To tell my story, there are, of course, other "players" in the game. Under no circumstance will real identities be revealed. Unfortunately, there will be some who will be outright pissed because "they know who they are"…that's if they choose to read this book. If they didn't like me before, they will really dislike me now.

I have come to learn there is a cost for freedom, a cost to remove the shackles, and a cost to living authentically. If I want to live—I mean **TRULY LIVE,** survive, and be the best version of **ME** that I can be—I must continue to move forward and do what's best for me. If I didn't, I would never know what my life's purpose entails!

So, to those who called me names like *"Red Bitch"*…to those who said, *"You think you're better than us"*…to those who ask, *"Who in the hell do you think you are, with your bougie ass,"* I would like to take a moment to thank you! Why? The answer is simple:

Had I not learned my value to the universe, I could be of no service to others if I didn't show up as my authentic self!

Writing this book was no walk in the park. I struggled like hell to get each and every single word out of me. Today, I am walking with boldness and in the purpose for which I was created. In order to walk in my purpose, I must do that which is painful.

Sharing some of what you will read herein is, indeed, painful.

At every turn, procrastination, fear, doubt, shame, and the horror of certain memories greeted me. I oftentimes found myself just sitting and staring at the computer screen, wondering what in the **HELL** I was doing. Time and again, the question arose:

ARE YOU SURE YOU WANT TO EXPOSE THE VERY THINGS THAT COULD CAUSE AN EVEN *GREATER* LEVEL OF REJECTION AND ABANDONMENT?

It took great courage, meditation, and lots of prayers to move forward word by word and page by page. I knew what needed to be done, and I worked tirelessly to accomplish the task.

Here's what I know to be true to get to the next season in life:

- ❖ There will be tests and trials.
- ❖ There will be things we **MUST** experience because, without them, the next season could very well be the one thing that knocks us off our feet…permanently.

So, with each season, I faced it head-on because of the awareness that it was **NECESSARY**. I had to be unequivocally prepared for the next season. There is an order to the healing process that must be adhered to for completeness, to include dealing with that past "thing" before going on to the next.

Penning this book was a part of my healing journey. I must release this because I will be unable to accomplish what's next until I am healed. I have no doubt this is meant for others as well.

Ask yourself: *What gift…what blessing is waiting on* **MY** *healing?*

One thing about me that holds true is this: I have never been one to pretend my way through life. I refuse to sit comfortably with the untruth of **ANY**thing. While I'm not the best at everything (yes, "SHE" made mistakes during her adolescent years through to today and sometimes fall short), I can promise you that *Chandelier & Suicide* is my authentic self showing up in the world. It is my sincere hope that on the pages of this book, you will see my story in such a way that you see yourself.

Know that it doesn't matter what you've experienced in life because, plain and simple, your story is far from over. Yes, life "happened" — making it a **PART** of your story but not the *END* of your story. Now, you can say **YES!** Now, you get to make the hard decisions!

Read my story and discover the warrior within **YOU!** Be encouraged! *EVERYTHING* you need to bring along with you on your healing journey can be found on the pages of this book as you begin to heal from the inside out!

Introduction

The year was 2013—one of my most difficult years to date. What I remember most about that time was how despondent and lonely I truly was. On the outside, the world perceived a happy "SHE." What "they" didn't know was that I had mastered the art of disguising my truth. In fact, doing so had become my "norm." If I were to be honest with both myself and you, I rarely operated from a place of wholeness for most of my life. Giving that state of existence a name, I have one word for it:

SURVIVING.

I failed to recognize I wasn't living my life from a place of wholeness. I seriously lacked a connection to my true identity. For far too many years, I functioned in my "norm." I would get up each morning, dress corporate-America style, and go to work—all while ensuring no one knew I had just spent the previous evening with the covers overhead, submerged in a flood of tears. On the inside, I was downhearted, downtrodden, and in state of constant despair.

As 2013 was coming to an end, so was I. My life had become more than I could bear. I no longer had the strength to fight the thread of lies I had been living. I likened my life at that time to a game of double-dutch—bossing back and forth, waiting for the right time to jump in. Often feeling anxious, I wondered:

Did I really have the strength to pursue the life about which I've dreamed?

It was apparent to me that my time on this Earth had come to its natural end. After all, my days were dark and lonely. Hope for brighter days was nonexistent.

As 2014 was approaching, I knew I couldn't spend any more of my days suffering from the overwhelming aches that plagued my soul. My desire to be accepted and loved was simply too engulfing.

The secrets.

The lies.

The abuse.

All the unanswered "WHYS?"
had finally won the battle.

I cried out to my God. Wait. Why could I no longer hear His voice? I **SCREAMED** out to Him, and all I heard were the echoes of my screams.

Okay. **THAT** did it! My brokenness had won. I finally threw in the towel. It was "confirmed" that my life was worthless. Why should I continue living with the weight of the anguish?

So, there I was…alone and preparing to do the unthinkable. Travel back in time with me as I share with you what led up to "The Unthinkable."

Table of Contents

Dedication vi
Prologue viii
Introduction xiii
SEASON ONE 1
   Grandmother is Calling! 2
   Tell Me the TRUTH! 6
   Abandoned 8
SEASON TWO 13
   Just Who IS My Momma? 14
   You Can't Pick Your Family 17
   SHHH! Don't You Say a Word! 20
   The Past vs. The Present 27
SEASON THREE 29
   My Son and Me 30
   Bagels and Cream Cheese 35
   New Furniture Was a Must 41
   Your Ride is Here! 44
   Keep it Together 48
SEASON FOUR 51
   Girl, Get On the Plane! 52
   An Envelope and a Ring 59
   He Needs a Green Card 61
   Enough of This! 65
   The Savage Beatdown 67
   Behind Closed Doors 71
   Gone For GOOD! 74
   I Don't Know Who I Am 79

FINAL SEASON	81
About the Author	83
Contact Sheila Malloy-Hall	85
Other Publications By and With Sheila Malloy-Hall	86
Suicide Prevention Resource	87
This is Your Time	88
Appendix	97

Chandelier & Suicide

Season One

Sheila Malloy-Hall

Grandmother is Calling!

The air in the house was filled with the scents of great cooking and small bursts of cleaning products. The chandeliers hung high and shone brightly down on all who graced the home. My grandmother would thoroughly dust the house every weekend, ensuring not a speck remained. Whenever she took notice that one of her antique drinking glasses lacked a sparkle, she would gently remove it from the glass China cabinet and give it a good cleaning until it shined like new.

My grandmother was an excellent cook and baker. Saturday mornings, I would awaken to the smell of breakfast permeating the home and the sound of my grandmother's voice asking, *"Sheila, you want something to eat?"*

"Yes, ma'am," came my reply.

I would make my way downstairs to the kitchen, and she would say, *"Get yourself something to eat. There is plenty!"* — and **PLENTY** there was! Before I fixed myself a plate, I would stand over the stove, look at the spread of food, and taste everything with a spoon. Double-dipping was a no-no in my grandmother's kitchen. I can still hear her admonish me:

*"I **KNOW** you're not using the same spoon to taste my food! Why don't you fix yourself a plate like a civilized person?"*

As I reminisce on those days, I find myself still shaking my head in confusion at her reprimanding. What does being civilized have to do with tasting food?

I cannot emphasize enough how amazingly delicious my grandmother's cooking was—and her buttermilk biscuits? They were to die for! I would add butter and jelly to enhance the flavor, but, in all honesty, they didn't need my help whatsoever. I was very fortunate to have a grandmother who cooked the most amazing food from scratch. I'm still in awe at how I never witnessed her measure a single thing. Talk about impressed!

So, for breakfast, I would load up my plate with eggs, bacon, home fries, fried apples, and, of course, the biscuits. Being mindful that I wanted to leave room for the Lemon Cream Coconut cake, I would enjoy a small portion of breakfast, all while eyeballing that cake. I would then slice myself a piece and make a fresh cup of hot coffee.

Life was truly beautiful.

I wasn't the only person able to enjoy grandmother's cooking; the entire family did. She always had a hot meal on the stove and a handful of desserts to choose from. The desserts were kept in the China cabinet in the dining room, as if they were on display for all to see—and what a sight it was!

Chocolate cake.

Lemon cake.

Flavorful pies.

(The bread pudding was kept in the refrigerator, but everyone knew it was there.)

Most evenings, one could find me in the kitchen with my grandmother as I watched her cook. I really enjoyed watching her chop, cut, and create but mostly, I loved the conversations we would have about food. I was over-the-moon happy when she would say, *"Come over here and help me."* She would spend that time providing great detail about her cooking. I promise you this: It was like watching an artist create their next masterpiece because **EVERYTHING** she cooked was just that. And the flavors? ***OMG!***

My grandmother wasn't the "hugging-kissing-type." I believe that was a consequence of her growing up in a family where love was rarely openly expressed. Over time, I learned her love language, which included the private moments we shared while laughing and looking out the window (we were the unofficial "Neighborhood Watch"). I don't remember her ever speaking the words *"I love you"* to me, but in my **HEART**, I know that she did.

The way she cared for me had to be love. The way she cooked for the family was filled with love that could be tasted in her delectable foods.

My grandmother could be just as sweet as her cakes and pies — especially towards me — but she could also be one of the meanest women on the planet. She had soft, fair skin without a wrinkle in sight. She was a very classy lady who always kept herself looking nice and polished. She didn't have to be going anywhere in particular; that's the way she was all the time — elegant in her ways. **BUT** the *MOMENT* you pissed her off or disrespected her, she would let you have it! All of that softness quickly vanished as she cursed you out and set you on **FIRE** with her words. She was fierce and no joke…and I loved her with all my heart.

Sheila Malloy-Hall

Tell Me the TRUTH!

T**RUTH** — *"Being in accordance with the actual state or conditions; conforming to reality or fact; not false"* (Merriam-Webster, n.d.).

Imagine growing up with burning questions that needed honest answers. Well, that was me. Questions abound, such as:

- *Why were there no pictures in the home of me as a baby?*
- *What sort of toddler was I? Funny? Quiet? Outgoing?*
- *What was I like as a little girl?*

I don't think it's unrealistic to want answers to those types of questions. In fact, I believe it's my birthright. Sadly, the answers never came. I had to remain in wonder about who baby, toddler, and little girl Sheila was. There is, however, one thing I heard repeatedly:

"*Sheila, when you were a little girl, you could curse like a sailor!*"

Now, why in the **WORLD** was **THAT** a funny story to recall? Apparently, I repeated what my grandmother would say. In the same vein, I was never fond of hearing them recall "the good, old days" and surely didn't think it warranted humorous moments at my expense. (Okay, maybe the first couple of times, it was funny, but after a while, I grew sick and tired of hearing it.)

It seems to me that the stories others seem to recall about my past make them sit back and laugh about my antics. The stories mean nothing to me because they left me with more and more questions about "Sheila the infant, toddler, and little girl." Somehow, the story-telling managed to skip my youthful years, and quickly progressed to stories of me being a spoiled brat and my grandmother's "pet."

Although there are many things I cannot recall about my childhood, there is one that puts a smile on my face. I tell it every chance I get!

I believe I was in elementary school at the time. I was in a school play and can remember dancing to "White Christmas" as I walked through the Winter Wonderland. I waved my hands from left to right and sang along:

"Gone away is the bluebird; here to stay is the new bird…"

I'm not quite sure those are the exact words to the song, but the memory brings me joy every time it crosses my mind.

The question remains, though: Why are my memories so few and far between? While I can recall other moments in time from my childhood, many are not **MY** memories but those of family members. From those conversations, I, in essence, built what I *perceived* to be an accurate account of my past.

The search for **MY** truth left me waking up every morning with a suspicion that there was something not being told. Were they withholding for my good? Perhaps that's what they thought—but they would be wrong.

Abandoned

ABANDON — *"To leave; completely and finally; forsaken utterly; desert"* (Merriam-Webster, n.d.).

Something **HAD** to be wrong with me because my mother gave birth to two children before me and two after, but I was the only one she left at the hospital. For many years, *"Something is wrong with me,"* echoed through my mind, much like a resounding echo in an empty house. To add to the conundrum, the fact that there were no childhood pictures of me seemed to confirm my thoughts. It didn't help that there was a plethora of stories that circulated about why my mother left me behind.

In my private time, I became obsessed with getting the truth and gathering the answers I so desperately needed. The woman in the mirror was always looking past me — as if I were transparent — constantly reminding me of my painful past and how I would never be able to go on living my life without her. I experienced some traumatic things that would lend themselves to the secrets I held close to me…the secrets that gave life to my state of brokenness.

It's funny to me how people get so excited about their birthdays. Now, I'm not saying I don't get excited about mine because I absolutely do; however, as it relates to the day I was birthed, I can't say there was anything special about the moment. Why is that, you wonder? The problem is I don't know anything about my actual birth. Many people can share the story of their "born day" as it was told to them, but as for me, I'm not that girl. All I can tell you is what happened a couple of days after my birth…as it was told to me.

From what I was told, my grandmother was the one who brought me home from the hospital. I had no clear concept that she wasn't my birth mother until the age of 12. Once the truth was revealed to me, I bore a load of unhealthy emotions:

- ❖ *Pain*
- ❖ *Shame*
- ❖ *Hurt*
- ❖ *Rejection*

That last one I carried for many years…***ALONE***.

What also pissed me off about that situation was that for many years, folks (primarily family members) had the damn nerve to make accusations and have opinions about how I should feel. As one who never dismisses others' trauma, I came to resent how so many people have told me to *"get over it."* I refuse to give anyone the power to dictate to me when the heck I will "get over it"! I have since learned that (generally speaking) people cannot get over any form of trauma without doing some healing work (something I learned after doing my own self-work).

I recall a time when my mother was standing on my grandmother's front porch crying and asking, *"Let me take my daughter home, Mama!"* My grandmother replied, ***"NO!"***—and reminded my mother that she left me behind and obviously didn't want me.

Not long after that incident, I started gaining more insight into who my mother truly was. I recall the day I sat in a room with my mother, grandmother, and a woman I didn't know. I vaguely remember a man being in the room as well. The adults in the room talked about me as if I wasn't even there! I remember hearing the name of my biological father for the first time. There were lots of tears shed, too. In the confines of that room, a decision was made that the unknown woman would take me home to live with her. I was both scared and confused.

As it turned out, I lived with that woman and her children in what became my foster home. I had no true understanding of what living in a foster care situation should feel or be like, but I must say that it was an amazing experience! I was comfortable in my new setting and felt I was supposed to be there. While others might have struggled with the newness of it all, I had no difficulties whatsoever. Once I moved past my initial fear, I was treated very well, loved, and became a part of the family.

It was during that season in my life that I began attending church regularly. Not only did I attend; I participated, began to understand the teachings of the Bible, and spent time in prayer. Knowing what it meant to be a Christian was a wonderful experience in my life.

When I was a preteen, I returned home to live with my grandmother. That arrangement came with an agreement to spend weekends with my mother.

One of the fond memories I have is from when I came across a photo of my mother in her young adult years. She was twenty-something, slim, and beautiful. To this day, I remain amazed at how much I resembled her.

Spending time with my mother and siblings had its set of challenges, but there were also fun, laughter, and exciting times. For my siblings and I, we missed out on those young years of bonding. As such, we began our sibling-bonding in our teens. I believe we all missed out on bonding in our childhood years. Nonetheless, I've grown to love them — and nothing could ever change that.

Free yourself from
the prison of others'
judgment of you.

Season Two

Sheila Malloy-Hall

Just Who IS My Momma?

As it was **FIRST** told to me, my grandmother received a call from the hospital informing her that her daughter checked herself out of the hospital and left her baby behind. (Over the years, I learned the reason why she left me — which I will share soon.) So, my grandmother brought me home and raised me as her own.

I remember one time, my mother came to my grandmother's house and, very shortly after, left with me (keep in mind that at the time, I didn't know the woman was my mother). I'm pretty sure my grandmother had no idea my mother intended to remove me from her home. I recall being so scared and yelling and screaming in the car to go back. I also remember "mother" yelling at me from the front seat and telling me, *"You better shut-up and stop that crying!"* Later that evening, I was returned to my grandmother's house, where an argument between the two women ensued. Unfortunately, that wasn't the first or last time "mother" defied the rules set forth by my grandmother.

Those moments in time were very upsetting for me and actually left me fearful of "mother." I vaguely recall her visiting my grandmother's home from time to time. Were the visits pleasant? I honestly cannot remember one way or another. Most times, the two women had conversations I couldn't hear or, in reverse, ones the whole neighborhood could hear. Each instance, I was the topic of discussion. "Mother" would oftentimes leave with tears streaming down her face. Although I wasn't fully aware of the circumstances, I felt connected to the pain and was often very sad.

When I inquired about what was going on—**WHY IS YOUR DAUGHTER UPSET ALL THE TIME, GRANDMA?**—I was told, *"Stay out of grown folks business."* That's exactly what I did.

TRAUMA — *"An emotional response to a horrific event"* (Merriam-Webster, n.d.).

Years later, I had a conversation with my mother in which she shared with me the difficulties she had with walking out of the hospital without me. She stated it wasn't easy to do and explained that she was a young mother with two children without the means to care for a third. Amid an argument with her mother, she was told, *"Don't come home with that baby!"* Well, my mother took that instruction to heart and left me behind.

It has taken me years to get to a place where I can honestly say I understand what my mother went through and forgive her. After all, fear makes people do things they would come to regret all the time. More importantly, I acknowledge that she did the best she could with what she knew. I can relate to her, as well. I, too, have made many mistakes as a young mother. I have no doubt she was broken, shameful, and experienced much trauma in her life. She was raised in a family where survival skills were much more important than the healing of the heart.

I've never shared the following with anyone, but I will with you because this is all about my healing journey…

I often thought, *"What would my life had been like were I adopted by a nice, wealthy family?"* I easily imagined growing up in one of the most influential neighborhoods with big, fancy houses. I would have worn the finest clothes, received the best education, and went on fabulous vacations.

Well, that obviously didn't happen. However, as I got older, I had the pleasure of meeting families I would consider "well-off," causing me to think, *"Oh!* **THIS** *is how life is supposed to be!* **THIS** *is how families are supposed to behave!* **THIS** *is how they are to treat one another!"*

Oh, but wait! Every family has their "stuff" — some level of ***dysfunction*** that is their normal. Some are worse than others. Thinking back, maybe my family was considered one of "the worst." I cannot state that with any surety, but I can say that every family is fighting a generational curse of some sort — a behavior that was passed down from generation to generation.

You Can't Pick Your Family

Our family was known for our cookouts and get-togethers. Our gatherings were more like block parties that everyone wanted to attend. If you lived on the block (and my grandmother liked you), you were welcome to join us. I am not exaggerating when I say that our parties were the place to be!

It was always nice having the family together. It was **ALSO** interesting trying to remember everyone's name. The celebration included the latest dances at the time (i.e., pop and lock, drop it low, the ever-popular Soul Train line, and hand dancing) to both classic and new music. Dancing was one of the things that connected us as a family — and I must say that we all could *DANCE!* Those were, indeed, the good old days!

FAMILY – *"Any group of persons closely related by blood, as parents, children, uncles, aunts, and cousins"* (Merriam-Webster, n.d.).

As for my grandmother, she did **ALL** the cooking. The menu was long:

- *BBQ chicken and ribs*
- *Fried chicken*
- *Hot dogs*
- *Hamburgers*
- *Potato salad*
- *Macaroni and tuna salad*
- *Seafood salad*
- *Corn salad*
- *Every kind of cake and pie you could imagine!*

Okay. You get the picture, right? And, just as mentioned previously, she cooked it all **FROM SCRATCH!** I can't forget to mention that the liquor bar was stocked as well. Many of my family members could outdrink anybody and often challenged others to a "drink-off."

The cookout would start in the early afternoon and last until either a fight broke out or somebody pissed off grandmother. When the latter happened, she would stop the music and tell everybody: *"Get the HELL out!"* Should someone attempt to challenge her decision, there was hell to pay! One of her children was bold once and said, *"Oh, come on, mom! Don't ask like **THAT**!"* Why, oh why did they do that? That enraged her even more, causing her to scream and yell — with a slew of curse words freely flowing from the very depths of her belly. If she were **VERY** angry, she would grab her baseball bat or the hatchet that she kept behind the front door for such an occasion. She was not afraid to show off that hatchet! When it made its appearance, we *ALL* knew the shit was about to get really crazy, and EMS would show up shortly after.

I don't recall hearing stories about someone being hurt by my grandmother's choice of weaponry. However, to this day, I don't believe my grandmother would have ever hurt any of us. She intended to scare the hell out of us…and it worked!

Our family cookouts were a time for bonding, connecting, and meeting new family members. Sadly, I also believe the gatherings became a way for some to settle old disputes. In their defense, I don't think they planned it that way, but a few libations gave some just the push they needed.

I imagine my family is not much different than others in that unresolved conflicts can prove extremely stressful. Within the family unit, the desire to trust one another is paramount, but with some members, trust is virtually impossible to obtain. In a moment of further transparency here, I must say that I've been disappointed with some of my family members—and I have no doubt some will say the same about me.

With all the love our family had, one might find it hard to believe that there was a great amount of discord in the forms of cursing and fighting one another. Not every gathering was disrupted by anger, but when there was liquor and drugs involved, the chance that all hell would break loose was ever-present. It never ceased to amaze me that a simple conversation would turn into an outright brawl. How humiliating it was to see a family fight like strangers.

HOW COULD FAMILY FIGHT EACH OTHER LIKE THAT AND CALL EACH OTHER SUCH AWFUL NAMES?

I have come to believe that each family fight had a negative impact on the younger generation that witnessed the adults' bad behaviors. Mental scarring has, indeed, affected **me**—and I have their actions to thank for the wounds.

SHHH! Don't You Say a Word!

SILENCE — *"The absence or omission of mention, comment, or expressed concern"* (Merriam-Webster, n.d.).

There are memories I wish I could erase—ones I wish never happened to me, but they did, and I couldn't continue to keep them to myself.

I grew up surrounded by strong women who had very dominating personalities. While they were very strong, I also believe there was a great deal of pain in their lives. Their strength caused them to do their best to hide those pains. As an adult, I now understand that they did so because of embarrassment, shame, and the ever-so-common familial understanding that simply states:

"You don't tell your family's business."

Most likely unintentionally, those generational behaviors were instilled in me as well. I, too, was a strong woman. I, too, hid my pain because of shame. I was always looking for something while having no idea what it was that I sought after. Confusing, I know.

What I came to realize early on in life was that I wanted more for myself than the load of pain I carried and kept hidden. The weight of my burdens was immense! I have no doubt the pain I bore was identical to the women in my family. You see, the women in my family possessed a strength that was meant to protect them and enable them to mask their brokenness. Just as I did, the women in my family longed for love, protection, acceptance, and freedom from the chains that held them captive and in bondage for far too long.

I was distressed and fearful for years because I wasn't sure how I would ever be able to tell my painful truth. As I got older, I heard more and more stories told by other strong women and realized I wasn't the only one. (I believe the older women in the family remained silent as they passed the torch from generation to generation of keeping family secrets, well…secret.) It's pastime for me to break the curse, **BE FREE**, and expose some awful truths!

SEXUAL VIOLATION – *"Committing physical violence against another, especially rape and sexual assault"* (Merriam-Webster, n.d.).

Sexual violation entered my life in the form of "The Pony Ride" that two of my male cousins "played" with me. Every single time the two of them were together, it was playtime. Each boy would take turns picking me up and then grab and wrap my legs around their lower waist. They would place both of their hands on my butt to hold me in position and say, *"Ride the pony! You like it?"* All the while, they would be laughing hysterically. Of course, I didn't understand what was happening at the time due to my young age, but I clearly remember being held and forced to play a game I didn't want to play.

The memory of "The Pony Ride" raised an anger in me that was glued to me for quite some time. It would haunt me during the day and invade my dreams at night. It put a fear in me because I didn't like the fact that they held me against my will. I was just a young child who didn't have a clue about sexual violations. In my naivete, I thought it was just a game. However, there was an unseen impact that seemed to all but stifle my growth: the game was continuously played in my life. Saying, *"No! I don't like this,"* while being forced to play the game took what little fight I had out of me.

I held onto that memory in silence so tightly because of fear. Why did they do that to me? Was it because they didn't know any better? Was it because they really thought it was fun? I never received answers to those questions—although, admittedly, I never asked. To this day, I have never revealed the names of the two cousins that violated me. I have decided not to divulge that detail. What's most important to me is that I chose to forgive them and pray they are now resting in peace.

"The Pony Ride" was the first time I experienced being sexually violated. Sadly, it wasn't the last. The next time, I was violated by an uncle. I must be completely truthful here and say that he is probably the second person I have disliked the most in my life. The experiences with "Unc" were horrible. What I know to be true is that I wasn't the only one he took advantage of. He destroyed lives in ways that no child—no **PERSON**— should ever have to deal with.

His behavior affected so many. What is so damn heartbreaking is that this family secret was "unspeakable." *How in the HELL do you keep a family secret like that?* As a consequence, the violator is protected from prosecution and free to continue violating others and exposing himself to children!

I won't apologize for how I feel about him. I didn't like him then, and I still don't like him now. I will say it again:

I. WON'T. APOLOGIZE. FOR. HOW. I. FEEL.

I was left with the residue of sadness, pain, trauma, and nightmares. How can anyone like (much less *LOVE*) a family member who has taken their vulnerability and used it for their own pleasure?

For whatever the reason, "Unc" was assigned to be my caretaker at times. Still today and even as I write this, I shake my head with disgust. What in the world would possess someone to leave a child alone in his care? What were the adults thinking?

He would take me into a room, lay on the bed, grab me by my waist, pick me up, and set me on the bed very close to him. Each move was very methodical. As the music played in the background, he would smile and bob his head to the beat — then begin touching himself on the surface of his pants. Not long after that, he would take my little hand and rest it on his growing male member, and then cover my hand with his giant one and massage his private parts. Without fail, he eventually unzipped his pants to remove and fully-expose himself to me. When that happened, my hand was no longer needed. He continued massaging himself while touching **MY** body with his free hand until he finally relieved himself.

Those types of instances happened countless other times with "Unc." Not once did anyone ever ask me about or make mention of his behavior. For the longest time, I wondered if they even suspected I was being sexually violated and, if they did, no one came to my rescue.

"Unc's" behavior was allowed to go on for so long, I personally hold **EVERY** adult accountable — **EVERY** person who knew what he was doing and did nothing about it. My message to you is this:

***YOU** bear the brunt of my pain because you all **KNEW** that man had mental issues. **YOU** chose to keep your mouths closed. **YOU** turned a blind eye to the abuse. **YOU** permitted that big family secret to destroy many lives.*

For many years, I kept the dirty, little secret buried deep down inside. I somehow knew I wasn't the only female in my family to be violated by some men in the family, but they, too, kept it to themselves. As for me, I was distressed for **YEARS**. I dressed up that pain, put makeup on it, and moved forward with my life. As I got older, I remember there being conversations among family members about his behavior — but what were **CONVERSATIONS** supposed to do? The females of the family needed **ACTION!** Talking about it and doing something about it were two different things.

"Unc's" choice of music was anything by Al Green. I recall that as he listened, he would bob his head in such a way that he appeared to be losing control of his mental faculties. I used to enjoy Al Green's music as well, but as soon as I realized I was enjoying the same music as "him," I would start to feel sick to my stomach. I would abruptly turn the song off or change the station…and then work vehemently to shake the horrific memories from my foremost thoughts.

The last episode I will share in this book about being sexually violated involved someone who made the violation considerably worse (in my opinion) than any others: a sibling. What made it even **MORE** disgusting and **MORE** horrifying was that he was caught in the act! What he did was no secret because—and I repeat: **HE WAS CAUGHT IN THE ACT!**

My sibling had knelt by the side of my bed as I was sleeping. He pulled the covers off my body, pulled my panties down, and began touching my vagina with his fingers. When I didn't stir out of my sleep, he inserted his fingers and had his way with me. I was awakened by the screams of a family friend who walked into the room as the molestation was happening.

In response, I began screaming and crying as the family member grabbed him by the sweatshirt he was wearing and yelled, *"WHAT'S WRONG WITH YOU?"* They then yelled for my mother to come into the room. My sibling took off, running downstairs and out the door before my mother arrived.

I sat on the bed crying hysterically, as the person who witnessed the event came over and held me in their arms. Once my mother made it into the room, she asked me if I was okay. I replied, *"Yes."* How could I say anything else to that question that lacked empathy? My **TRUTH** was that I *WASN'T* okay, but I knew no other way to respond.

Let me backtrack for just a brief moment. Earlier that day, I was involved in an awful accident that left a scar on my right leg that is still visible today. That incident was the reason why I was upstairs sleeping as hard as I was. Well, that molestation incident was the final straw. I never visited my mother's house again.

Sadly, I carried a hatred and anger that burned my soul because nothing was done about it. Although my sibling was not in his right mind at the time (he was under the influence of drugs), that is **no excuse** for the lack of concern displayed by the adults in my life.

The Past vs. The Present

There were many times when I felt like my past had an impact on the present. It seemed I harbored a great deal of anger and resentment for a very long time. I also believe abuse, depression, and trauma plagued my family. It became apparent to me after some time that my family members did not know how to exercise coping methods (if any of them even knew what those methods entailed).

I also wonder if the stories I have heard have anything to do with the infighting and anger that ran rampant through each generation. While I am sure alcohol and drugs played their part, I am thoroughly convinced the hurts and pains were labeled as "unforgivable." Their stories were my stories, too. I have no doubt any of us wanted to take ownership of our horrid pasts, but that was the hand we were all dealt.

In our silence, the women in my family collectively manifested the deep-rooted pains that we had in common but refused to openly share with others. The adults nurtured the darkness, and the same became true for me in my youth.

As for the men in the family, they were known as the "strong, silent type." However, they were not without their own set of shameful issues—not *ALL* of them, but certainly one or two. As I close out this season, I'm left to wonder what that "thing" is that happened to them that caused them to act out the way they did.

Sheila Malloy-Hall

Some say that silence exhibits control. On the contrary, that isn't always true. From my experience, I can attest to the fact that sometimes, silence means that truth is hidden.

Season Three

Sheila Malloy-Hall

My Son and Me

As a refresher of my relocation history during my youth: I went from…

- *Grandmother*
- *To foster care*
- *To mother*
- *Back to grandmother*

I was 18 years old when I gave birth to my first child. The scariest moment during that pregnancy was having to tell my grandmother that I was pregnant. **TALK ABOUT BEING NERVOUS OUT OF MY MIND!**

I was so ashamed and felt awful because, in some ways, my grandmother was very protective of me. I imagine it's because she assumed the role of mother when I was practically fresh out of the womb. As such, the very idea of disappointing her brought me great sorrow.

The day I told her the news, I reluctantly went into her bedroom and saw that she was seated in her favorite place: a chair to the right of her bay window. She often sat in that exact spot so that she could keep an eye on what folks were doing in the neighborhood (remember I said she and I were the unofficial "Neighborhood Watch").

As I approached and greeted her, I immediately took notice that she had a "knowing" expression on her face. She instructed me to have a seat. I pulled up a small storage suitcase and did as I was told. She turned toward me, gave me her undivided attention, and asked, *"What's wrong?"*

IMMEDIATELY, my heart skipped a beat. From the moment I learned I was pregnant, I practiced over and over what my exact words to her would be. It was time to put them out there into the atmosphere…*and I wasn't ready.* I dug down deep into the pit of my voicebox and finally found the strength to tell her three simple words:

"Grandma, I'm pregnant."

As I sat there, I braced myself and waited for the tongue-lashing to come flying out of her mouth, expressing complete disappointment in me, but that didn't happen.

Instead, she just looked at me and then at my midsection. It was as if she could see the baby in my uterus! Breaking the deafening silence, she said, *"I know you're pregnant."*

Wait. How could she? I didn't tell anyone who would dare share the news with her before I did!

She continued. *"Does the baby's daddy know that you're pregnant?"*

"Yes, he does." That brought on a flood of tears. I began apologizing to her, sobbing uncontrollably.

"What are you crying for? Were you crying when you were making that baby?" Classic grandma. She sure had a way with words!

There wasn't a thing I could say in response because anything I would have said at that moment would have been misconstrued as me trying to be a smart mouth. There were many things my grandmother would say that you automatically knew you were **NOT** supposed to respond to. Now that I think about it, it was often best not to reply to *ANYTHING* she said when you were in the wrong.

My grandmother made it very clear to me that carrying the baby full-term and giving birth was the **ONLY** option.

Again, I was left speechless.

So, my circumstance had certainly changed. I was 18 years old, in the 11th grade…and pregnant. At that time in my life, my life was running in neutral. I was neither happy nor sad about my situation. My unborn child's father knew I was pregnant and, for the most part, was thrilled; however, he was young himself, in college, and already had a family of his own.

When my son was born, my world changed yet again. It wasn't just me any longer; I was responsible for a little person who didn't ask to come into this world. In many ways, he saved my life. His arrival forced me to look at my life through a different lens. No longer was I able to be concerned solely about me, me, me. Each time I looked at my child, I envisioned a better life for him, which required me packing away all my hurts, pains, and shames to be and do better for him.

I believe our children deserve nothing but our absolute best. After all, **WE** chose to carry them. **WE** chose to give birth. **WE** chose for them to exist in this world (abortion was never an option for me, remember?). Although some of us may not have had the advantages we desire to provide our children due to circumstances out of our control, we must give ourselves credit for fighting our way through. At the very least, we owe our children the gift of our best selves—even if all we ever knew in life was a hot mess.

My first apartment was a small, one-bedroom in a four-unit building. I was so excited! I had my own place! Life was all about my baby boy and me. While I was overjoyed about my new beginning, I was also stressed and unsure of myself. I had big dreams for us and promised my son that his life would be much different than mine was for most of my time on this Earth up to that point.

MY SON would know that he's loved.

MY SON would know he was always wanted.

MY SON would know his mother wrapped him in a blanket and brought him home from the hospital.

MY SON would know the story of his birth as told by **ME**.

As life would have it, stressful moments came. When they reared their ugly heads and had me feeling as if I was literally suffocating, I would pack up my son, get into the car, and go for a long drive. I loved getting into my car and driving for an hour or two with no destination in mind. I would turn on the music and let the sound "take me away." *Who needed Calgon when I had my son and a blue Ford Escort?*

Looking back, I realize just how blessed I truly was. The family that lived downstairs from us was also a single-parent household; a mother and three daughters. Our like-circumstances created an unbreakable bond, and we became family. Her daughter babysat my son, we shared food, and what one didn't have, the other did. We spent a lot of time running up and down the stairs to each other's apartment. I used to think that when I moved out on my own, I would be all alone. I am grateful to God for His ram in the bush. Thinking about those days brings a warm smile to my heart.

It was important to me that I created happy memories with my son. As a young mother, there was so much I wanted to give him, but I had no idea about the level of meeting his needs first entailed. I was right back into what I've always known—survival mode—and I was determined to do whatever it took for us to make it!

Bagels and Cream Cheese

My first job! How exciting! I had a feeling of accomplishment, unlike anything I'd known before. I began to plan what I was going to do with my first paycheck. I envisioned all the trips I would take with my son, the new clothes I would buy for him, and the new furniture I so desperately needed.

The **MOST** exciting thing about that time was that we were getting ready to relocate to a much bigger and nicer place! As the Jefferson's would say (but with my little twist):

"We were moving on up!"

I remember my first day on the job. I was a receptionist at a law firm. I was a ball of emotions, with fear and excitement taking the lead. Well, excitement got the best of me because the sense of independence was my new reality. I had an apartment, a job, and was making a life for my son and me. I was finally prepared to put all the bullshit behind me. What I'd gone through and all those pains of the past didn't matter one iota at that moment.

My first day on the job consisted of being trained on the switchboard and learning how to answer the phones professionally (if I must say so, I did **VERY** well on my first day). One of the things I like most about me is that I have great communication skills—which is saying a lot for a black girl who grew up in Northeast Washington, D.C.! Oddly enough, no matter how professional and articulate I spoke, I could not shake my D.C. accent!

As time progressed, I found myself getting along well with my coworkers. I started hanging out and going to lunch with them. It was then that I had my first bagel and cream cheese—and I loved it! During our time together, my new acquaintances would discuss their experiences in life. I spent more time listening than talking because their walk was not quite like mine; their truths were not mine. The one similarity I shared and happily engaged in conversation was that my family was one that sat around the dinner table discussing education and planning for the future. For the most part, it appeared everyone had amazing stories about their childhood and families they were eager to share…but not me. I didn't look forward to those types of discussions **EVER**. When I did participate, I was very strategic about what I said. I must be honest here and admit that I sometimes told bits and pieces of a life I wished I had. Any time I shared, my coworkers seemed to find it interesting, as proven evident by the nods and smiles. That gave me the boost of confidence I needed to divulge only what I wanted them to know and nothing more.

Many thoughts and priorities were competing for my attention, but I needed to stay focused on the one thing that would keep me feeling good and focused: my son. I had a responsibility that was greater than me. As time went on, I decided to go to school. I had a passion for "all things beauty," as it was one of the things that made me feel very comfortable, so I enrolled in beauty college.

Life was good! I was working a full-time job, going to school in the evening, and my son was receiving the best of me.

My confidence steadily grew, and I was genuinely excited about the future for the first time.

Of course, there were bumps and bruises along the way, but with every challenge, I remained focused. Even when I had a slip-up now and then, I didn't allow the disappointment to overwhelm me. Those things I experienced were nothing in comparison to what I faced in the past. My resolve to do **MORE** than survive encouraged me all along the way.

Then, the day came when I had a meltdown.

I remember it well. I was in class when suddenly, anxiety grabbed me by the throat and wouldn't release its hold. Doubt began to set in, leaving me unsure if I could accomplish all that I had planned. Right there in front of everyone, I broke down and bawled my eyes out. I must have looked like a crazy woman to those around me at the time. I'm very thankful for my ever-present God and the people He uses to bring forth clarity and practice patience. My hair instructor came over to me, took me by the hand, and guided me to her office. Once seated, she handed me a tissue and gave me a moment to collect myself.

Once I moved past being embarrassed, a calming sense of relief enveloped me. I was blessed to have someone who cared about me in my brokenness. My instructor asked, *"Do you want to talk about it?"*

"No, thank you."

"Do you want to go back to class?"

I replied, *"Maybe in a moment. I'm sure everybody's going to be staring at me like I'm crazy."*

"It's okay," she said with surety. *"If everyone stares at you, they're probably staring at me, too!"* We then shared a laugh and returned to class.

After that incident, I made an appointment to see my doctor. On the day of the appointment, I completed the necessary paperwork and was eventually called into the examination room. When my doctor entered, she asked, *"So, what brings you here today?"*

I told her I was having moments when I felt anxious and overwhelmed, leading me to cry at the drop of a dime. Sometimes, I wasn't even sure why I was crying. Other times, I felt panicked and afraid.

Just as my instructor did, the doctor asked, *"Is there anything you want to talk about? Did anything, in particular, happen that you can think of?"*

I took a moment to think about that second question. My **TRUTH** was that so much had happened! Was it possible the doctor could sense something about my past? Was that why she asked me if something happened? Maybe she knew…but, how could she?

When I finally returned to reality, I looked at her and said, *"No. Nothing happened. Well, nothing bad anyway. I just don't know what's wrong with me."*

It was then I was diagnosed with an anxiety disorder and prescribed medication. The first couple of weeks were very trying for me. I felt awful while taking the medicine, but the doctor said I needed to take it as prescribed so that it could get into my system. I did as I was instructed and returned for a follow-up appointment two weeks later. At that time, we talked a little bit about how things were going, and then she again asked me what was on my mind.

Paranoia set in. Did she know my deep-seated secrets? Did she know what happened to me? Was I walking around with a **"DAMAGED GOODS"** stamp on my forehead that only she could see?

Nonetheless, my stoic response is what I gave her: *"No, nothing happened. I just don't know what's wrong with me."*

She didn't press the issue but suggested I speak with a therapist. I replied, *"I don't want to talk to a therapist. Can't I just talk to you? You're my doctor. I'm not comfortable talking to anyone else."*

"Okay, but please think about it."

Those types of appointments continued for quite some time, as she continued to monitor my progress while on the medication. For the most part, I was feeling okay. There were the occasional anxiety attacks, but I would shake them off and fake it until I made it.

I pushed myself to show up at work and school on schedule. I really didn't have anyone else to rely on, so I had to make it happen for my son and me. All the while, I lied and covered up the pain that was haunting me. There were times I relived episodes from the past, but I knew I still couldn't tell anyone about them. It was necessary to keep hiding my secret. Assuring others that everything was okay became my normal. I repeated those words so much, I came to believe my own lie.

New Furniture Was a Must

When I answered an ad for a 2-bedroom condo, I met with a woman who was the manager of the building. Instead of viewing the condo I had originally gone to see, she showed me a different one that was owned by her. That condo was actually much nicer, and the square footage was astonishing. After sharing with her a little bit about me being a working single parent, she gave me a good price on the rent.

All new furniture was a must! I needed a fresh start in my new environment. I thought to myself, *"A little sparkle and shine would do the trick!"*

My new job afforded me a salary where I could buy all new furniture. I was determined to make our new home even better than the first. I was thrilled to live in a condo and started shopping almost immediately. I put so much love into decorating because I wanted—**NEEDED**—a new "feel" mentally for my son and me. I was head over heels in love with our new home and couldn't wait to put up our Christmas tree with my famous cookie treat for Santa (that became a family tradition).

One of my first major purchases for the home was a chandelier I found at a consignment shop. I paid someone to remove the light fixture that was in my bedroom and install the chandelier. (Okay…it wasn't exactly a chandelier, but it was a very beautiful light fixture that upgraded the look of my room.) Things were finally going well, and we were off to a great start.

I was so in love with all I was learning in beauty school. When the course started teaching about skincare, my interest was piqued. In response, I chose to pursue a degree as an Aesthetician. I continued working full time while attending school. I was laser-focused on creating a better life for my child, and obtaining a job as an Aesthetician was just the thing I needed.

After graduating, I began working as a full-time Aesthetician in a salon in downtown D.C. As part of my routine, I would stop by one of the fancy coffee shops downtown, grab a cup of coffee, and make my way into the salon. Coffee seemed to be the drink of choice for my peers, and I wanted to fit in, so I adopted the coffee-drinking culture.

While working at the salon, I had a mixture of both male and female clients. I was even afforded the opportunity to service a few "local celebrities," such as a makeup job for Dr. Dorothy Heights and a massage treatment for Kathy Hughes. I was in my element and loved everything about the beauty industry. I also worked part-time with different cosmetics lines, and, before I knew it, the creative side of me began to blossom.

Although I was enjoying my life and experiencing peace, there were still times at night when I dealt one-on-one with insomnia. I had difficulty resting my mind due to an overwhelming sense that something was wrong that was of the utmost urgency. I could not afford to give my past pains the attention they needed and, consequently, my spirit remained uneasy.

On one particular occasion, the night had come and gone. It was time for me to get up, get dressed, and head into work. I arose, turned on some music, and began my day. Music had become my therapy. I did, after all, grow up with the sounds being ingrained into my very being. When I listened to music, it warmed my soul. The rhythm spoke to me and made me feel so good. Every instrument could be heard in their uniqueness. I often imagined myself as a ballerina, tap dancer, or even a modern dancer. In my world, I felt strong and brave. I would feel such a high level of energy that everything would be peaceful, warm, and happy. As I went about the business of preparing for the day, music helped me set aside anything that ailed me.

So, what I thought would be a typically busy day at the salon turned out to be anything but. One of my clients was gorgeous (that would be the first time I ever referred to a man as "gorgeous") and he smelled delicious! As I greeted him and introduced myself as his Aesthetician, he looked at me as if he was expecting someone else. When I asked if everything was okay, he replied, *"Yes. You're an unexpected surprise!"* I remember feeling the eyes of all the women in the spa shooting darts at me. The gentleman had an appointment to get a deluxe facial treatment. No wonder his skin was so damn gorgeous! He was a man who clearly took good care of himself!

Your Ride is Here!

A couple of days later, I received a delivery at the spa: two dozen roses with a card that read, *"Don't underestimate your worth."* My first thought was, **"Wait! Does he know me?"**

About three months or so, he returned for another treatment. That time, he was a bit more casually dressed than the first time when he was all suited up. I remember one of the women at the salon come back to the treatment room and say, *"Mr. Gorgeous has arrived."* After exchanging pleasantries, I thanked him for the flowers and began his treatment.

While applying his mask, he opened one eye, looked up at me, and asked me to have dinner with him. I declined the invitation. After several months of him persisting, I accepted his offer. He sent a limo to pick me up and, of course, my mind was blown. **THAT** was a first for me! After dinner, we went to a party (he called it "a gathering with some business associates"). Upon entering the house, a server greeted us with champagne. As we walked deeper into the main room, **"WOW!"** was all I could say. Even the *people* looked luxurious. The event was the most elegant gathering I had ever been to up to that point. I had never seen anything like it. It had the most beautiful, shiny chandelier, and immediately, I knew I had to have one of my own!

The home, the people, the food, the artwork, and the aroma in the air…that is what I wanted for myself. As the lady of the house gave me a tour, I thought, *"I want to live just like this."*

Eventually, I made my way into a room where my date for the night and several other people were. When I looked down at the table where they were gathered, I noticed they were all snorting cocaine. I just stood there—dumbfounded. My date beckoned me and said, *"Here, baby. Have a seat with me."* As soon as I sat down, he asked, *"Have you ever tried this?"*

I shook my head and replied, *"No."*

"Well, let this be your first experience with me." I watched him snort a line and then followed suit. I thought nothing much of it because I was having such a good time. I chose to participate in the festivities and enjoy the rest of the evening. The ride home, however, changed everything between us.

At one point during our journey back to my house in the limo, he began passionately kissing me. It was like Heaven on Earth...until he started trying to undress me. I stopped him from progressing and said, *"Stop. The kissing is fine, but you're not undressing me."* When he asked what the problem was, I firmly stated, *"I'm not having sex with you."*

"What the hell do you mean 'you're not having sex with me'? Of course, you are!"

A lot more assertively, I said it again: ***"I'm NOT having sex with you!"***

I could see the darkness cloud his eyes at that moment. He grabbed me by the throat and said, ***"You WILL have sex with me when I tell you! Do you understand me?"***

I was terrified and didn't know what to do. Should I fight? Do I scream? Or do I follow his orders?

He obviously felt he had the upper hand and began undressing me again. I had an overwhelming feeling that screamed, *"I DON'T WANT THIS!"* My fight or flight response kicked into overdrive, and I started to fight. I screamed, *"GET YOUR DAMN HANDS OFF ME!"* I asked the driver for help, but he turned the music up. There would be no help coming from him. My date and I tussled in the back seat until he wrapped both hands around my throat and said, *"Bitch, I should kill you! Do you know who I am?"*

I had no fear in me when I replied, *"Then you should fucking kill me because I am **NOT** having sex with you!"* I started screaming like a madwoman. The next thing I knew, the car came to an abrupt stop. The driver opened the door, and my date said, *"Bitch, get out of my car."* As I got out, it was then I realized I was half-dressed. In my hysterics, I didn't realize I was let out in front of my building. I quickly gathered myself and quietly went inside.

Once behind the safety of my closed and locked door, I fell apart and cried painful tears. I knew I was a mess—both mentally and physically. I didn't have the strength to get my son from the sitter, although she lived in the same building. I needed time to get myself together, so I let him stay the night with her.

That experience broke me. It took me to a dark place where I vividly recalled every catastrophic thing that ever happened to me...every dark moment. How could I have let that happen? How could I have been so naïve? I thought that man cared about me and was just being kind, but I was wrong.

The remainder of the night seemed to drag on and on. My thoughts were out of control, and my heart was hurting. Could it be possible that perhaps my birth was a mistake?

As soon as daylight came, I went to get my son and put the tragic events of the night before behind me. I wouldn't dare let my son see me falling apart.

Sheila Malloy-Hall

Keep it Together

The next morning, I called my doctor to make an appointment. I told the receptionist it was urgent and that I needed to see her immediately. I was told to come right in.

By the time my doctor entered the room, I was extremely emotional. Over the years, she and I had established an amazing connection. As a matter of fact, she had become almost like a best friend to me because I could tell her things that I would never tell anyone else. Still, there were some secrets I had yet to share.

"What's wrong, Sheila?" she asked. I could tell she was very concerned about my wellbeing. I then told her about the tragic evening I had. One of her main concerns was whether he and I had sex. I told her we didn't but also told her about and showed her the bruises he left on me. She stated she wanted me to report him to the police and would be there with me when they took my statement.

"No. I absolutely am not going to do that," I said sternly.

After going back and forth for a moment, she finally let go of the issue and realized I was not going to call the police. She gave me some time alone while I cried tears of great pain. When she returned, she asked me a direct question:

"Have you ever experienced anything like that before?"

Without even thinking about it, I told her the truth. *"Yes. When I was younger, a man touched me inappropriately and forced himself on me."* I then opened up and told her about the experience I had with my uncle. For the remainder of the visit, we talked about that experience, but I quickly shut down because I was outright exhausted by then. I just couldn't share anything more.

It was then that I received an epiphany when the doctor said, *"The trauma of your childhood and holding it all in is having an impact on you. You need to tell me about whatever else is going on."*

I couldn't share anymore. In hindsight, I probably shared too much. I had gone as far as I was willing to go. Still, I must give credit where credit is due: The doctor was on point when she said the secrets were taking their toll on me.

Before I left the doctor's office, she wrote me a doctor's note excusing me from work. She instructed me to take a few days off to mentally rest and to return to see her before my vacation. She again spoke about referring me to a therapist, and I agreed to make an appointment—but not before telling her that I had yet to get comfortable enough to talk to anyone else about the events of my life. After all, I didn't trust anyone else but her. As usual, she assured me therapy would be good for me.

Meanwhile, I was trying my hardest to be the best me I could be for my son. I worked both full- and part-time, enrolled him in basketball camp, dressed him well, and read him bedtime stories. We had long talks about black history, I took him to the doctor on schedule, and made sure he took pictures on Picture Day at school. I did everything for him that wasn't done for me in my youthful days. In my mind, I thought I was making it better for him, but something still felt wrong. Perhaps he needed more than just a mother. Maybe he needed his father full time. Since I didn't grow up with my father, that was part of the pain I endured. I didn't want that for him. Although I was trying by giving him everything I didn't have, I remained overwhelmed.

I made a decision that literally broke my heart, but I knew it was necessary. I permitted my son to go live with his father and spend weekends with me. He needed to be with his father. He needed to have a consistent male figure in his life. He needed and deserved stability. Those were the things I told myself to help ease the pain.

What I didn't know back then was that I was just running from my pain, trying to break free from the agonizing shackles that were attached to me. I found out later that there was only one way to deal with it.

Chandelier & Suicide

SEASON FOUR

Sheila Malloy-Hall

Girl, Get On the Plane!

"*What a beautiful home!*" Those were my exact words when I walked in the door. The homeowner was a striking woman, elegant, articulate, and well-dressed — and her beautiful home was to be my new residence.

I never thought I would move back into the city. I had invested so much time moving away and, to my surprise, was excited to be back. My new roommate and her beautiful home were mind changers. Her house was the type that I dreamt of living in and raising my child.

I loved the home! It was so beautiful and quite expensive-looking, if I must say so. The homeowner and I bonded immediately. With the age difference between us being a potential issue, I was pleased to learn that although she was a little bit more uppity and educated than I, her inner-beauty shone through brightly. She was just a regular, older woman who was living her best life. I have no doubt she had her own set of challenges, but I tend to believe they were nothing like what I had suffered in my young life.

She and her family accepted me as part of their family. What a blessing it was! I settled in and lived comfortably. My son visited most weekends, but the consistency was slowly but surely waning.

Sometimes, she and I prepared dinner together and engage in wonderful conversations. I shared my dreams with her, and she advised, *"Do what makes you happy! You don't need permission from anyone to be happy."*

One night when we were having dinner, my roommate stated she was going on vacation in a couple of days. When I asked her where she was going, and she said, *"Bermuda,"* I had no clue what she was talking about.

"Where is Bermuda?" I asked.

She began to tell me about the island and then out of nowhere, asked me, *"Would you like to come?"*

I had never been on a getaway vacation before, so I was all in! Then it hit me: I had never been on a plane before, either. I was terrified but knew I had to accept her invitation — so, I did!

Before going away, I needed to check in with my doctor. She repeatedly asked, *"How are you?"* It brought me great joy to be able to say with **HONESTY** that life was truly fantastic!

"Why is life fantastic?" she pried. *"What happened? Please share!"*

"Well, I moved and have a fabulous roommate. I'm preparing to go on vacation outside of the country, and the most exciting part is that I'm getting ready to board a plane! I've never done that, and I am **EXCITED***!"*

"That's awesome, Sheila! I'm happy for you. A vacation will do you well. Have you given any more thought to seeing the therapist?" I was hoping she wouldn't ask **THAT** question. I assured her I've given it thought and would pursue her

suggestion upon my return. *"How are you doing with the medicine?"*

I lied. *"Just fine."* The **TRUTH** was I stopped taking the medicine because I didn't think I needed to take it anymore. I was feeling pretty good, and my past was no longer plaguing my every waking hour. I had moved on. Why I lied, I cannot explain.

When it was time to take our vacation to Bermuda, I was **READY** to go! The flight was relatively short as we soared across the ocean to our destination.

~~~~~~~~~~

OH MY GOD! I have never seen a more amazing place in my life! The pink beach and turquoise water were absolutely gorgeous and inviting! We stayed at her godmother's beautiful home. I was welcomed with open arms, which made me feel right at home. She had prepared a delicious lunch for us: salt cod, potatoes, Black Rum cake, and champagne. (I had never eaten salt cod before, let alone heard of it, but it was very tasty.) Once we finished eating, we rested a bit and had a great conversation. We then made plans to go out later that evening.

We went to a charming place that was like a dinner club. Everyone was very nice, the music was fantastic, and we were having a good time. I then noticed someone from the bar was watching me. Right before I could lock eyes with him, a waiter approached us and said, *"Here are two drinks from the gentleman over there."* It was the same man who had been watching me.

My roommate and I looked at each other, said **"Cheers!",** and enjoyed the champagne.

Shortly after, the man who sent the drinks over walked up and introduced himself. We responded in kind. Immediately, he knew we were not from Bermuda because neither of us sounded nor dressed like a native Bermudian. We must have stood out like a sore thumb.

He joined us, and we had a delightful conversation. I thought to myself, *"He seems innocent enough."* During our chat, my roommate made it very clear that we had family on the island. When she mentioned the family name, he acknowledged that he was familiar with them. Pretty much everybody knew one another or was related to someone on the island. (I think he got the unspoken message that he **BETTER NOT** start trippin'.)

He stated he wanted to "show me Bermuda"—his island. I explained that it was my first time visiting and that my roommate had visited several times, so I wanted her to show me around. He, however, persisted and wanted to take me sightseeing to show me the island from his perspective. We exchanged phone numbers, and he asked me to call to let him know when he could take me out.

The next morning, as we were having a lovely breakfast, we discussed the night before. My roommate insisted that I tell our host about the gentleman we met. When I mentioned his name, she said she recognized it but wasn't quite sure who he was. The host asked, *"Are you going to go out with him?"*

"I don't know," I said. "I don't know him like that."

"Oh, please! I believe I know his family's name. He's not crazy enough to do anything. He's probably a really nice guy. I think you should go. Do you have his number? You can have him pick you up here at the house like a perfect gentleman, which will give me time to ask him a couple questions about who his family is and where he lives."

Well, that's exactly what happened. He picked me up, introduced himself to our host, and had a brief conversation with her. We then went out and had a great time. He took me all around the island and showed me things I probably would've never seen if I was just a tourist. Before dropping me off, he asked if he could see me again. He said he enjoyed himself so much with me that he just **HAD** to see me again before I left his island. I replied, *"Absolutely!"*

A couple of days later, we had dinner. It was a wonderful moment in time for me. He was handsome, charming, mild-mannered, and innocent. The meal was delicious, by the way. Who would've thought a girl from the streets of D.C. would experience such an event after all I had gone through in life?

I told myself it was time for my past to die. All that I had gone through was finally behind me. I was in a better space mentally. I just needed a change of scenery. Life was truly grand!

As I laid on the beach's pink sand and had the warm water envelop my feet, my healing began. Bermuda was my therapy. The breathtaking experience was so new and quite refreshing. While in that place, I felt as if I had reached a part of me deep inside that I never knew existed. It felt so good! I loved what I felt and just knew that was what life is supposed to be about. After listening to my old coworkers at the law firm talk about their amazing vacations, my prayer had been answered. I was on my dream vacation!

Growing up, my family never discussed vacationing, let alone a trip to the Caribbean. Up until that trip, I had never been outside of the DMV or even seen pictures of exotic places. I wasn't sure if it was normal to be as excited as I was, but I couldn't help myself! I really psyched myself out to believe that my life was all better now, thanks to that one trip outside of the country.

Weeks passed by since our return trip home. I often reminisced about the time away on the beautiful island, the peace I felt, and the pleasant gentleman I met. It was apparent he thought about me often as well because he called me constantly. He also wrote me letters, sent cards, and occasionally had flowers delivered. It was a lot like a long-distance relationship that I didn't realize I was involved in at the time.

Once home, it was time to get back to "life" as I knew it. I wasn't dating anyone. As a matter of fact, I hadn't gone out with anyone since that last horrible date. I had secluded myself and decided to focus on me. Mr. Bermuda was a welcome distraction, although there were parts of me that remained skeptical. I couldn't figure out why he was so interested in me.

With him across the water, what harm could be done with flirting, phone calls, letters, and cards?

Before I knew it, he and I began discussing him visiting me. We had several conversations about it, and a couple of months later, I picked him up from the airport for his visit.

He seemed to be that same, charming man I met on the island. He was thrilled to see me and, I have to say, I was excited to see him again, too! I was to be his tour guide and take him around "my city." I remember when I took him home, my roommate asked me, *"Are you sure it's a good idea to have him come visit you?"*

"Why not? He seemed very pleasant to be with in Bermuda."

She sighed and said, *"Okay. I'm getting ready to leave on another vacation."* (She often traveled and truly lived her life.)

Everything seemed to be happening so fast with him and I. I would fly back and forth to see him, and he would do the same. In between, the letters, cards, and flowers kept coming. I was enjoying life and went along for the ride. Not once did I think anything terrible would happen.

An Envelope and a Ring

Months later, he asked me to marry him, and I was happy about it. I didn't tell anyone except my roommate and her mother. I remember her mother saying to me, *"This is a bad idea, Sheila. This is not good. I am afraid for you."* I couldn't begin to comprehend what she was saying. Why did she say such a thing? Couldn't she see that I was happy?

There was a problem I had, though. Did I really know what love was? Was what I felt true love?

One day, I received a FedEx package on my job from him that contained two envelopes. One was stuffed with cash; the other held an engagement ring.

Who does that? Who sends $3,000 cash and an engagement ring through a COURIER SERVICE?

At the time, I was in shock and wasn't thinking clearly. I quickly hid the envelope with the cash, placed the ring on my finger, and showed it off to all the girls in the salon.

Once I broke the news to the women at the salon, they were so excited for me. I told them all about the wonderful man I met in Bermuda and was getting ready to marry him. They even bought my wedding bouquet, styled my hair, and celebrated the occasion with a small bridal shower at the salon.

Only one person knew when we were going to get married. He and I went to the Justice of the Peace to have our nuptials performed. The only person there with us on that day was my aunt. She celebrated my happiness and said, *"If this is what you want, then I will support you."* I really didn't feel like I could tell anyone else. I was, after all, still bothered by the comment made by my roommate's mother that my getting married was a "bad idea." I slept with those words and woke up to them—but I got married anyway.

Right after the ceremony, we went out to dinner and then returned home to our new apartment. There was no time for a honeymoon because I needed to get back to work.

Let me backtrack again for just a moment. Yes, you read that correctly; "our apartment." While doing the long-distance relationship 'thing' and leading up to us getting married, I told him I had to find an apartment for just the two of us because he couldn't move into where I was living when we met.

He Needs a Green Card

We had a really nice apartment on Pennsylvania Avenue between Capitol Hill and Southeast D.C. It was a furnished basement apartment and was quite charming. Weeks later, he said to me, *"You need to get a new car."* Apparently, driving my trusty Ford Escort wasn't fancy enough for him, so I purchased a two-door Ford Probe. It was white and sporty — and he loved it!

While I worked, he stayed at home. He wasn't able to get a job because he needed to get a Green Card to work legally in the U.S. (that was something I discovered **AFTER** we married).

In between clients, I spent my days in the salon calling the Immigration and Naturalization Service gathering information on how to get him a Green Card. I also contacted the Social Security Administration to find out how he could get his social security number. I know, I know… They were things I should have spent time doing **BEFORE** marrying him and having him come live with me. In my defense, I had no clue about the complexities of him gaining citizenship. What I did know was that it was frustrating, exhausting, and overwhelming.

I remember one evening, when I got in from work, he asked me question after question. *"Did you call Social Security? Did you do this? Did you do that?"* I looked at him and said, *"Yes, in between being on the phone all day and working with my clients, I am **tired**."* Apparently, he found my response to be very disrespectful and offensive.

"What are you saying, Sheila? Am I a **BURDEN** to you?"

"No, that's **NOT** what I'm saying. It's just exhausting. I have to do my job and make money to pay the bills," came my exhausted reply.

"You **ALSO** need to tend to my needs so that I can get a job! Do you think I want to be dependent on you?" The tone of his voice was one I'd never heard before. However, I excused it away because I understood he was frustrated. I, too, was frustrated, so I ended the conversation by trying to assure him that I was doing everything I could to help him.

As time went on, I began to see a different side of him. He seemed to be angry all the time. Nothing I said or did was right. I purposely didn't get my son every weekend because the tension between my husband and I had changed the peaceful environment I had worked too hard to create for us. Things between us didn't feel right, and I didn't want my son to be in a situation I was no longer even sure of myself.

Going to the salon every day and working with my clients discussing skincare brought me great joy, but something was wrong. My joy was quickly evaporating. I was exhausted all the time and didn't engage others in conversation like I used to. When I had the energy to converse, I didn't want people asking me questions or probing. For example, when someone would say, *"You don't seem like yourself,"* I was easily offended.

Truth be told, I believe the offense came from me realizing my truth: **I WAS CHANGING.**

I spent my days trying to figure out ways to make him happy. When I returned home in the evenings, nothing I did worked. He was miserable. I equated his misery to him missing his family and being homesick. Often, he would make me feel bad by saying that he gave up everything to be with me. *"How dare you make me feel bad for not having a job!"* he would say. That was never my intention. In fact, I don't even know what he was talking about because whether he chose to acknowledge it or not, I was the one making the countless phone calls on his behalf! It didn't help to learn that the process to get him naturalized could take a year or more.

Every day seemed to come with its own dysfunction. One minute, everything seemed to be okay; the next, all hell would break loose. It was as if I was on a rollercoaster ride, going up and down, around and around, spinning out of control. I felt completely out of touch with reality and didn't know what the hell was happening to my life. I knew I needed to survive the guilt I carried. He somehow manipulated me into thinking I was doing something wrong and that I was the cause of the craziness. In between the craziness, we managed to have some fun times, though.

I remember the times we hung out with my family. They weren't the best experiences either because my brother wanted to jack him up. I don't think that would've been a fair fight. I'm sure my brother would have seriously hurt him, so I knew I had to get him away from my people. I came to realize I had no choice but to keep him and my family separated. Was it possible they sensed that something wasn't right with him?

Then, there was the day I came home from work utterly exhausted. I wasn't in the mood for his bullshit. I resolved early on in the day that I wasn't going to continue being mistreated, yelled at, and cursed at for no real reason. The arguments we had were horrible.

What in the hell did I do? Why in the hell was I working so hard to try and stop my past from destroying my present or future? I had gone completely backward. I wasn't even seeing my doctor or taking the anxiety medication anymore.

Enough of This!

That night, when I walked into the apartment, I looked at him with disgust. I could feel in the air that there was going to be a bad episode. The air was thick with tension—so thick, I started to turn around and run right back out the door. I should have listened to my gut instinct that was trying to guide me. Sadly, I wasn't in touch with that part of myself yet.

I walked into the room and asked him, *"So, how was your day?"* What I didn't know immediately was that he decided to go out and buy a bottle of liquor, so he was inside drinking all day with his frustration building. The apartment was a mess, too.

Instead of answering my question, he tossed one back that shocked me: *"Where have you been?"*

*"What are you talking about? I've been at **work**."*

*"Why are you coming home late today? **WHY ARE YOU LATE?**"* he screamed accusingly.

"Sometimes, I run a little late. I do, after all, work two jobs. I don't appreciate you questioning me like this," I replied venomously. *"What is it that you want from me? I work two jobs, drive a nice car because you wanted me to have it, I give you my paycheck just so you can feel it in your hands, we sit down together and pay the bills, and I **STILL** let you make decisions that a man should make.* **What the hell do you want from me?"**

The next thing I knew, I was in a defensive stance. I ducked and put my hands above my head because he was about to hit me upside my head with the iron. Suddenly, he stopped midstride, picked up the phone, called his mother, and said, *"This bitch is crazy! She's frustrating me and mistreating me!"* I heard his mother on the other end of the line say, *"Calm down. It's okay. Let me speak to her."* I stood there looking at him like **HE** was crazy. **Did he just say I was mistreating HIM?** He yelled into the phone, *"No! You don't need to talk to her. What do you want to talk to her about?"*

Once I snapped out of my moment of disbelief, I started yelling. *"LET ME TALK TO YOUR MOTHER! LET ME TALK TO HER!"* When he gave me the phone, I yelled, *"I DON'T KNOW WHAT'S WRONG WITH HIM? HE'S ACTING CRAZY!"* He then grabbed the phone from me and disconnected the call.

"Shut the hell up, Sheila!"

I looked at him dead in his eyes and said boldly, *"YOU shut the hell up!"*

The look he had in his eyes let me know that I was in trouble and needed to run for my life. I turned around and could see the front door from the bedroom. In my mind, I was screaming, *"RUN SHEILA! MAKE IT TO THE DOOR AND GET THE HELL OUT OF THERE!"* As I started to make my move, he caught me and pulled me down to the floor. I screamed for him to get off me as he pinned my arms down. I put up my best fight…until his fist connected with my face.

The Savage Beatdown

While at the salon, I found myself hiding out in one of the treatment rooms pretending I was preparing for the next client. In reality, I spent that time crying, praying, and asking myself, *"What in the hell have you done, Sheila?"* I was terrified and didn't know what to do.

Should I tell someone what was happening to me at home?

Should I tell someone about the fights and constant threats?

Should I tell someone about his mood swings?

Should I reach out for help?

I was so ashamed and completely lost. The more I thought about it, the more I determined I **COULDN'T** tell anyone about my situation because I had spent so much time lying and acting as if everything was just fine. How could I tell anyone that he slaps, kicks, bites, and punches me? Do I dare open my mouth to tell them he bites and throws me around like a rag doll? No. I couldn't tell a soul.

If I were to be asked, *"Why do you stay, Sheila?"*, I would have to reply, *"Because he apologized and cried remorsefully. Then, we would have sex and, while in the act, he would promise it would never happen again — and he would say it like his life depended on it!"* Would I just need to accept that abuse was the hand I was dealt?

When I didn't have a client, I sat in the treatment room and contemplated my life. How could I continue living like that? Over time, things had gotten progressively worse. I was scared out of my mind daily.

Eventually, someone would break through my thoughts by knocking on the treatment door. *"Sheila, are you okay? Your next client is here."* I would then do what I did best: gather myself and respond, *"I'm fine. All is well. I'm okay. Here I come."*

"I'm fine."

"All is well."

"I'm okay."

I repeated those words over and over again. I thought that perhaps if I said them repeatedly, they would somehow be my truth. I worked so hard to make myself believe they were true. Besides, since I've said that everything is okay for so long, surely, no one would believe the truth if I told them.

Well, I couldn't keep my clients waiting! In actuality, servicing them with a facial, massage, or other treatment gave me peace due to the relaxing environment in which I was submerged at the moment. Calgon, take me away!

~~~~~~~~~~

Note the different types of abuse:
Physical, Sexual, Verbal, Psychological, and Financial

~~~~~~~~~~

As I tried to catch my breath, I realized I was in the bathtub. I couldn't see my hand in front of my face because it was pitch black in there. I climbed out of the tub and felt my way to the light switch to brighten the room. When I flicked the switch and turned to look in the mirror, all I could do was cry.

He had beaten me severely and carried me to the tub afterward. As I surveyed the damage done, I saw that both of my eyes were swollen, but my left eye was swollen shut. There was blood everywhere, caused by the cuts and bruises on my face and body. I could barely breathe.

I made my way down the hallway, stopping briefly to look into the bedroom. He was there, laid out on the bed. He appeared to be asleep, so I tiptoed my way in and began searching for something to wear.

I managed to get my hands on a sheet to wrap around me as I searched for my clothes and shoes. From the corner of my "good eye," I saw my car keys. I quickly and quietly got dressed, grabbed the eyes, climbed into my car, and started driving. To this day, I can't begin to tell you what that drive was like. I don't even know how I drove in the condition I was in. I do, however, believe my Guardian Angel was working overtime that night.

Now that I think about it, if, indeed, my angel was with me then, why didn't they prevent the abuse?

Again, as the story was told to me, I made it to my mother's house. I have no clue how I even conceived in my mind to drive there. (There are still parts of my life that remain a mystery to me, and this is one of them.) My mother said that she heard a thump on her front porch. When she looked through the peephole, she didn't see anything, so she headed back upstairs. Something told her to turn around and look again. That time, she opened the door, and there I was—blood-covered and laid out on her front porch.

The police and EMS were called, and I was taken to Georgetown University Hospital in D.C. in critical but stable condition. I vaguely remember being questioned and examined. I had no clue about all that led up to the beating. I clearly recall being in excruciating pain, though. I'm unsure how long my hospital stay was, but I was eventually released and ended up going home with my mother.

The detectives questioned me the night of the incident, and I had nothing to tell them because I simply couldn't remember. Where was my assailant? Where had he gone? Once I was able, the detectives drove my mother, aunt, and me back to my apartment. When we arrived, there was the customary yellow crime scene "Do Not Cross" tape strewn all over the place. I was in a state of disbelief. One of the detectives advised against me going inside because they were still collecting evidence. I didn't listen. I went in and **OH MY GOD!** What I saw was an absolute nightmare! What in the hell happened in there?! We quickly gathered a few of my things while the detectives spoke with my neighbor who lived upstairs.

She told them she heard me screaming, but she was afraid for her life. She was so terrified, she called and taxi and got out of dodge. I don't blame her. She was a young college student with her whole life ahead of her.

Behind Closed Doors

Time stands still for no one. Months went by, and my life had been turned topsy-turvy. I was still living with my mom, trying to figure out what to do next. How ironic was it that I ended up with my mother again after a horrific experience? Although my memory is vague, I am thankful to God that she was there for me the night I arrived on her doorstep.

The police told me that my assailant somehow made it back to Bermuda. They contacted the authorities there and made them aware that he had been charged with "Assault with the Intent to Kill." If he **ever** came back to the U.S., he would be arrested on sight. His mother was made aware of the situation as well.

After speaking with him and his mother over the phone for a couple of months and after I accepted all of his apologies, he eventually returned—accompanied by his mother. No one knew I was secretly having conversations with his mother. It was she who convinced me that he was terribly sorry and that he was homesick and drunk at the time of the incident. She begged me, *"Please, please forgive him. He is so sorry and remorseful for what he did to you."*

Well, I did just that. Yep, I let him come back. Don't judge me. Don't even try to understand my choice…because I can't.

When he returned, he was, indeed, arrested. However, I did such an amazing job at convincing the court not to prosecute him, they dropped all the charges. What did I say? I cannot recall, but whatever it was worked.

When he was released, we moved into our new apartment. His mother stayed with us for a couple of months (I suppose that was to make sure everything was going to be okay). The following must be noted here: At that time in my life, I was totally isolated from everyone and everything I'd ever known. What little bit of peace I once had while working at the salon was gone as well. Everything in my life had changed once again. I was completely, utterly engrossed in life with him after his mother returned home.

Then, I found out I was pregnant.

That revelation didn't stop the abuse. I was still being beaten. I had jumped out of windows and a moving car. I'd been hit in my face with plates. I was choked and strangled into unconsciousness. I've been through it **ALL**. I was too terrified to leave him…and too embarrassed because I actually allowed the abuse back into my life. Maybe I deserved that life. Sounds crazy, right?

I do recall one time I called the police on him, but because there were no bruises, they offered us advice before leaving me at the apartment with him. Advice? Really? **ARREST HIM!** That didn't happen.

I spent many evenings contemplating suicide. It was almost as if he knew what I was thinking because he would say to me, *"Don't try anything stupid,"* followed by a threat against my son.

I was trapped with nowhere to go. My family and friends had no idea where I was. No one knew where I was working. No one knew how to find me. What kept me alive was the child I carried in my womb. When I learned via an ultrasound that I was carrying a girl, that changed my world. I was willing to accept the abuse because my unborn child gave my life meaning—a reason to live and combat the death I felt deep inside.

I was okay with accepting that my life was miserable and that I would eventually die, but I was fully awake and had to live for my baby. I spent most of my days with my hands on my belly, talking to my ever-growing child. Even when I cried because of an argument or a fight, it didn't matter to me. Touching my belly gave me comfort. It was my way of escape from reality. Yes, my life was horrible, but that bit of happiness that was growing inside of me kept me alive and gave me hope. I would do whatever it took to survive for my baby.

Eventually, I gave birth to a beautiful baby girl who was the joy of my life, my reason for living. The children I brought into this world were deserving of a **WHOLE** mother. It was their birthright to have something better, and it was **MY** responsibility to see them through.

Sheila Malloy-Hall

Gone For GOOD!

It is said that blessings come unexpectedly. I, for one, can truly testify to that.

My routine was the same: He would drop me off at work (he wasn't working) and pick me up when I got off. On this one particular day, he didn't pick me up on time. I called and called…and called. Eventually, something told me to call home and listen to the messages on the answering machine. I was shocked when I heard a woman's voice calling out for him to come open the door!

So, while I was at work, he was at home entertaining another woman. Honestly, that didn't even bother me. I couldn't care less.

Since I couldn't reach him, I called the babysitter. No one answered her phone, either. I then called my friend, explained I was stranded for the past two hours, and hadn't heard from him. I went on to explain that I desperately needed to get home to pick up my daughter from the babysitter's house. She and her husband came, picked me up, and we made the first stop at the babysitter's house.

When I was dropped off at home, I wasn't at all prepared for what I found. I turned the key and opened the door to an **EMPTY APARTMENT!** All I could do was laugh at first. I then ran from room to room and saw that *everything* I owned was **GONE.** The *only* thing I had was the clothes on my back and my baby girl.

I managed to release a genuine sigh of relief. ***WAS HE REALLY GONE FOR GOOD? WERE MY DAYS OF TERROR FINALLY OVER?***

The weeks seemed to fly by with no sign of his return. One day, I received a call that blessed my life. It was from a woman who lived in West Virginia—an estimated 300 miles away from where I lived. The caller stated she had found a bunch of trash bags with clothes, shoes, and other essentials. As she was going through them, she found a purse with my business card and decided to call me. I remember driving to West Virginia to see exactly what it was that she found. To my surprise, all of my belongings were there! **EVERYTHING** I owned was in those black trash bags. There was so many of them! All I could do was cry and share a bit of what happened to me with her. She said she was happy the items were able to be returned to their owner. I then loaded up my car, offered her some money (that she didn't take), and thanked her before driving away.

Sometime later, I moved into another apartment with my children.

~~~~~~~~~~

Eventually, I heard from him again. Come to find out, he was more conniving and sneakier than I ever realized. He had gotten his Green Card with the assistance of someone who had the same name as me. The "other" Sheila Malloy had signed all the necessary documents needed by the Immigration and Naturalization Service. Well, it was final. He could live and work in the U.S. legally.

I was pissed! Did he *really* think he could abuse me and then use **MY** name to stay in **MY** country? I was enraged and ready to *FIGHT*…or so I thought. After conversing with my attorney and reflecting on the pain and suffering I endured (and was still going through), did I **REALLY** want to be in that man's presence?

In the end, I chose just to let it go. I really didn't have a choice in the matter because I have no doubt had I pursued forgery charges, doing so would have dragged me deeper into the hole. At the time, I was already financially scarred (aka **BROKE**), depressed, and suicidal. I *HAD* to let it go because I had someone else to think about.

Just as I had done all my life, I was willing to sacrifice who I was or who I thought I could be. I had to at least **TRY** to forget what I had gone through in the past. I needed to find my way back to normalcy because my baby girl deserved my all. Setting aside everything tragic, I realized my baby needed me…and I needed her.

I soon got back up on my feet and got my own place again. Although there were ups and downs and mistakes made, it was important to me that my children were able to participate in activities that allowed me to live vicariously through them. There were times I robbed Peter to pay Paul to make it happen, but I did it!

I had grown accustomed to no longer giving my pain, shame, and hurt the time of day. I avoided them like the plague! When I had those moments when my past tried to creep into the present, I would fight it off. I refused to let what happened to me prevent me from enjoying special times with my children. In fact, I had some fun times of my own here and there by engaging in adult activities and building new friendships.

No one knew my secrets, though. I was so good at keeping them.

What "they" didn't know was that in the midnight hour, I would be wide awake, pacing the floor, and crying a **LOT**. As I watched my children sleep, I often shed tears because I struggled with whether or not I was even good enough to be their parent. Was I providing what they both needed and deserved? Behind the scenes, I was so sad because the past pains kept having their way with me. Every day, I had to battle unseen forces to be happy. I became an "Expert Pretender."

From time to time, I thought about myself. What about what I deserved? What about **ME**? I was talented and creative but also broken. I struggled with gaining an identity that was mine and mine alone, not what someone or something else used to define the very essence of "SHE."

~~~~~~~~~~

In my search for identity, I started the doctor-recommended therapy. I shared with the therapist just about everything but kept the deepest secrets of being sexually devalued unexposed. No way was I going to share with a virtual stranger my family's secret! (In the back of my mind, the words *"Don't tell what goes on in this house"* echoed repeatedly.) After all, no one else was talking about it, so I had to stick with the routine. The therapist tried to delve into that aspect of my life, but I refused those discussions. Instead, I would divert the conversations to those things I was willing to share.

What I failed to realize was that I would come to suffer tremendously for **not** telling my whole truth. Covering up things for people who didn't give a damn about me caused me to question myself. *"What in the hell is wrong with you, Sheila? Why are protecting those who didn't protect you?"* In hindsight, I acknowledge it was a deep-seated fear that screamed, ***"If you tell the truth, something bad is going to happen to you!"***

As a consequence of my "vow of silence," my self-confidence was dead. I wasn't living at all; I was just existing.

I Don't Know Who I Am

Now that you are aware of the pains of my past, allow me a moment to return to that dark place I mentioned previously for just a moment. I promise to bring you back to safety.

~~~~~~~~~

On that dreadful day near the end of 2013, I exhaled, cried, and finally committed to acting on a thought that haunted me for most of my life: I was going to commit suicide. I decided the easiest way to end my life would be by hanging.

As I stood on a chair with an extension cord around my neck, I began to reflect on my life:

- Abandoned as an infant
- Molested as a toddler and teen
- Abused and left for dead during my first marriage

There was **NO** way I could continue living such an unhappy life.

It was time to end the misery. With one end of the cord around my neck, I struggled with getting the other end into the vent from which I was to hang. After trying for far too long, my efforts were unsuccessful, and I was outright exhausted. It should not have been **THAT** difficult! I removed the cord from around my neck, climbed down off the chair, and fell to my knees. I cried uncontrollably and asked God to help me. I clearly heard Him say, *"YOU SHALL LIVE."*

The next couple of hours after that are a blur. I do know I had experienced something completely foreign to me. At the same time, I no longer felt alone. With the last ounce of inner-strength I had left, I mustered up the courage to release the pains that had manifested in other areas of my life due to the deep, dark secrets I kept hidden within my soul. As daylight began to break through the windows, I rose from the fetal position I had balled myself up into and stood tall. I basked in the experience of God and recalled both His promise to me and my promise to Him (I promised I would share my story with those to whom He assigns me).

The time for healing had finally come. I acknowledged God had called me to my next chapter — one where I would experience a closer walk with Him and a level of freedom, unlike anything I could have ever imagined. At that moment, it was revealed to me that my past was **STILL** showing up in my present — the life that was filled with trauma and fear.

Through my awakening and with God's grace, I wanted to **LIVE**! I wanted to live a different kind of life, begin my healing journey, and be free of the mental and physical abuse once and for all.

With determination, courage, faith, and professional support, my personal Healing 2 Grace journey began. Today, my journey continues; however, I use the lessons learned to inform, inspire, and encourage others to choose a life that is free from abuse and domestic violence. I desire to embolden others to be filled with health, joy, purpose, and empowerment.

Chandelier & Suicide

Final Season

Thank you for taking this journey with me and being a part of the seasons in my life. I couldn't bear to give you the details of every situation I overcame, but I gave what I could. I have learned I need always to be aware of my capacity to never try and reach beyond that just to satisfy someone else's insatiable need to "know."

Today, I am **BLESSED** to say I'm beginning to understand my identity and that it is not attached to anyone else. I am creative and have great potential.

As you have read, my journey wasn't pretty. Those ugly moments were truly horrendous. My prayer is that you get (at minimum) this one takeaway:

*You have the power to regain **YOUR** power.*

As for me, I don't intend to give mine away ever again. Yes, my journey continues — with ups and downs and turnarounds along the way. One thing I know for sure is that I hold the keys to my power and destinations as I continue to unwrap my full potential and my calling!

I can do ALL things through Christ that strengthens me!

About the Author

Sheila Malloy-Hall operates with many accolades. Tenacious. Enthusiastic. Humorous. Motivated. Spiritual. Domestic Abuse Survivor. Conqueror. The Chief Operating Officer (C.O.O.) of her life—just to name a few. These and more are characteristics of this Inspirational Speaker, Survivor Strategist, Advocate, and Author!

Sheila is the Founder of Healing 2 Grace, Inc., a 501(c)3 nonprofit organization that addresses the impact and aftermath of abuse and domestic violence. Healing 2 Grace, Inc. is a product of Sheila's personal and practical experiences. She knows all too well what it feels like to be powerless, shameful, broken, and silent. Today, she has taken back ownership of what the enemy thought he had the right to possess—her voice—and she speaks to her audiences from a place of power and humility. Her goal is and has always been to encourage and empower those who have been or are being exposed to abuse, domestic violence, and other traumatic life experiences.

As Sheila embarked on her healing journey, she encountered "broken" people who appeared to have it all together on the outside but have been adversely affected on the inside. She can relate because she used to present herself in the same manner due to the invisible scars of abuse.

As a woman of faith, Sheila remains candid and straightforward about her healing journey. As a Best-Selling Author, she has penned her unique truths to empower others by letting them know complete healing and restoration is possible—if they hold on just a little while longer. To that end, Chandelier & Suicide tells of her tumultuous past-turned-purpose. Her head-on approach with her coaching and training services continues to spur countless individuals to achieve lifelong transformation in their lives.

Sheila's dynamic message brings her audiences full circle; from tragedy and heartbreak to a place of hope and abounding joy. Her mission is twofold: to help one person at a time seek the help they need **AND** to do so unapologetically!

Contact Sheila Malloy-Hall

www.sheilamalloyhall.org

www.healing2grace.org

Facebook: www.facebook.com/Sheila.healing2grace

Instagram: www.instagram.com/malloy_h2g/

Twitter: www.twitter.com/healing2grace

Email: smalloy@healing2grace.org

Other Publications By and With Sheila Malloy-Hall

30 Day of Affirmations and Inspiration: From the Heart of a Survivor

Soul Talk – Volume 2: Soul-Stirring Stories of People Who Let Go and Let God

Available for purchase at:
www.sheilamalloyhall.org/books

Suicide Prevention Resource

National Suicide Prevention Lifeline
Call 1-800-273-8255
Available 24 hours every day

Online Chat
https://suicidepreventionlifeline.org/

This is Your Time

You may feel defeated. You may be in an abusive situation and believe there's no way out. You may have left an abusive situation and don't know what is in store for your future. It is freeing to begin journaling about whatever your situation, as it provides an opportunity to think freely and clearly.

The following section is all about **YOU**. You are under no obligation to share it with me or anyone else. *HOWEVER*, if you would like to share, reach out to Sheila Malloy-Hall through www.Healing2Grace.org.

Write your heart out…and then write some more!

YOU ARE NOT ALONE— NO MATTER WHAT YOUR ABUSER SAYS!

Chandelier & Suicide

Sheila Malloy-Hall

Chandelier & Suicide

Sheila Malloy-Hall

Chandelier & Suicide

Sheila Malloy-Hall

Chandelier & Suicide

Sheila Malloy-Hall

Appendix

Abandon. (n.d.) Retrieved July 17, 2019, from https://www.merriam-webster.com/dictionary/abandon.

Family. (n.d.) Retrieved July 17, 2019, from https://www.merriam-webster.com/dictionary/family.

Sexual violation. (n.d.) *American Heritage® Dictionary of the English Language, Fifth Edition.* (2011). Retrieved July 17, 2019, from https://www.thefreedictionary.com/Sexual+violation

Silence. (n.d.) Retrieved July 17, 2019, from https://www.merriam-webster.com/dictionary/silence

Trauma. (n.d.) Retrieved July 17, 2019, from https://www.merriam-webster.com/dictionary/trauma

Truth. (n.d.) Retrieved July 17, 2019, from https://www.merriam-webster.com/dictionary/trauma

Sheila Malloy-Hall

www.ingramcontent.com/pod-product-compliance
Lightning Source LLC
Chambersburg PA
CBHW052158110526
44591CB00012B/1992